SPORTS
STARTERS

Batter Up
Baseball

Bobbie Kalman & John Crossingham

Crabtree Publishing Company

www.crabtreebooks.com

SPORTS STARTERS

Created by Bobbie Kalman

Dedicated by Hadley Dyer
For Rachael Dyer, my little big sister.

Editor-in-Chief
Bobbie Kalman

Writing team
Bobbie Kalman
Hadley Dyer

Substantive editor
Kelley MacAulay

Project editor
Michael Hodge

Editors
Molly Aloian
Kathryn Smithyman

Photo research
Crystal Foxton

Design
Margaret Amy Salter

Production coordinator
Heather Fitzpatrick

Consultant
Tom Valcke
President and CEO
Canadian Baseball Hall of Fame & Museum

Illustrations
All illustrations by Trevor Morgan

Photographs
Chicago Gems Women's Baseball Club: page 17
Fotolia.com: © Charles Kaye: page 11; © Terry Poche: page 9
Icon SMI: Andy Altenburger: pages 25, 29; Mike Carlson: page 23;
    Jay Drowns/TSN/ZUMA Press: page 27; Mark Goldman: pages 14-15;
    Ron Schwane: page 26; Aaron M. Sprecher: page 19; Ray Stubblebine: page 24;
    Scott D. Weaver: page 28; Jeff Zelevansky: page 10
iStockphoto.com: Rob Friedman: page 31; Manuela Krause: page 13 (top);
    Matt Matthews: page 21
© ShutterStock.com/Tony Robinson: page 18
Other images by Corbis, Digital Stock, and Photodisc

Library and Archives Canada Cataloguing in Publication

Kalman, Bobbie, 1947-
    Batter up baseball / Bobbie Kalman & Hadley Dyer.

(Sports starters)
Includes index.
ISBN 978-0-7787-3136-8 (bound)
ISBN 978-0-7787-3168-9 (pbk.)

    1. Baseball--Juvenile literature. I. Dyer, Hadley II. Title.
III. Series: Sports starters (St. Catharines, Ont.)

GV867.5.K34 2007   j796.357   C2007-900587-X

Library of Congress Cataloging-in-Publication Data

Kalman, Bobbie.
    Batter up baseball / Bobbie Kalman & Hadley Dyer.
        p. cm. -- (Sports starters)
    Includes index.
    ISBN-13: 978-0-7787-3136-8 (rlb)
    ISBN-10: 0-7787-3136-7 (rlb)
    ISBN-13: 978-0-7787-3168-9 (pb)
    ISBN-10: 0-7787-3168-5 (pb)
    1. Baseball--Juvenile literature. I. Dyer, Hadley. II. Title. III.
Series.

    GV867.5.K36 2007
    796.357--dc22
                                                        2007002699

Crabtree Publishing Company

www.crabtreebooks.com   1-800-387-7650

Published in Canada
Crabtree Publishing
616 Welland Ave.
St. Catharines, ON
L2M 5V6

Published in the United States
Crabtree Publishing
PMB16A
350 Fifth Ave., Suite 3308
New York, NY 10118

Published in the United Kingdom
Crabtree Publishing
White Cross Mills
High Town, Lancaster
LA1 4XS

Published in Australia
Crabtree Publishing
386 Mt. Alexander Rd.
Ascot Vale (Melbourne)
VIC 3032

Contents

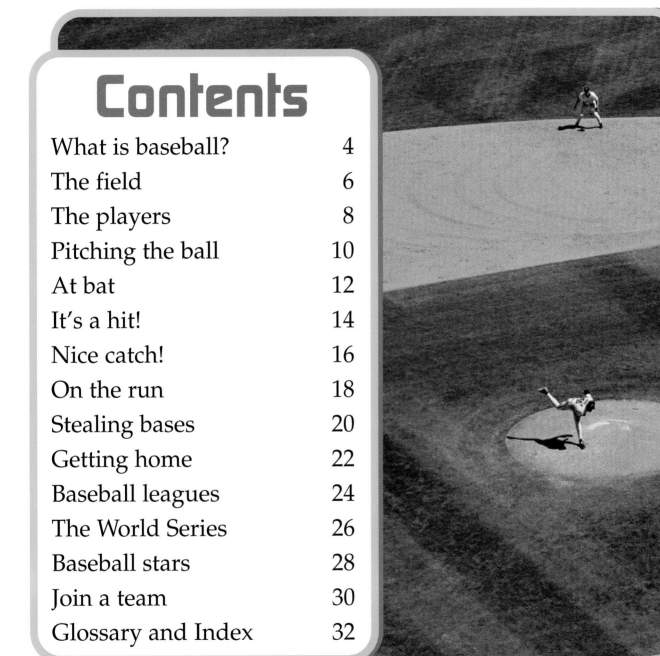

What is baseball?

*This **batter** is about to hit the ball.*

Baseball is a **team sport**. In a team sport, two teams play against each other. Teams play baseball on a large field. The teams take turns **batting** and **fielding**. When a team is batting, the **players**, or teammates, try to score **runs**. Players score runs by hitting a baseball with a bat. They then run and step on three **bases** and **home plate**. Each run is worth one point.

Fielding

When a team is fielding, it tries to stop the batting team from scoring runs. The fielding team stops the batting team from scoring by **making outs**.

Taking turns

There are nine **innings** in a baseball game. During each inning, a team bats once and fields once. The batting team bats until three of its players get out. The teams then switch places. The new batting team bats until three of its players get out. Then the inning is over.

Each baseball team has nine players.

The field

A baseball field
has two areas.
The two areas are the
outfield and the **infield**.
The outfield is the grassy area
outside the **baseball diamond**.
It ends at the wall or fence that
surrounds the field.

Baseball diamond

The infield is the area
between the three bases and
home plate. The three bases
are **first base**, **second base**,
and **third base**. Home plate
is where the players bat. It is
where they score runs, too.
The infield is also called the
baseball diamond because
the bases and home plate
form the shape of a diamond.

left fielder
(see page 8)

Foul lines *mark the*
sides of the outfield.

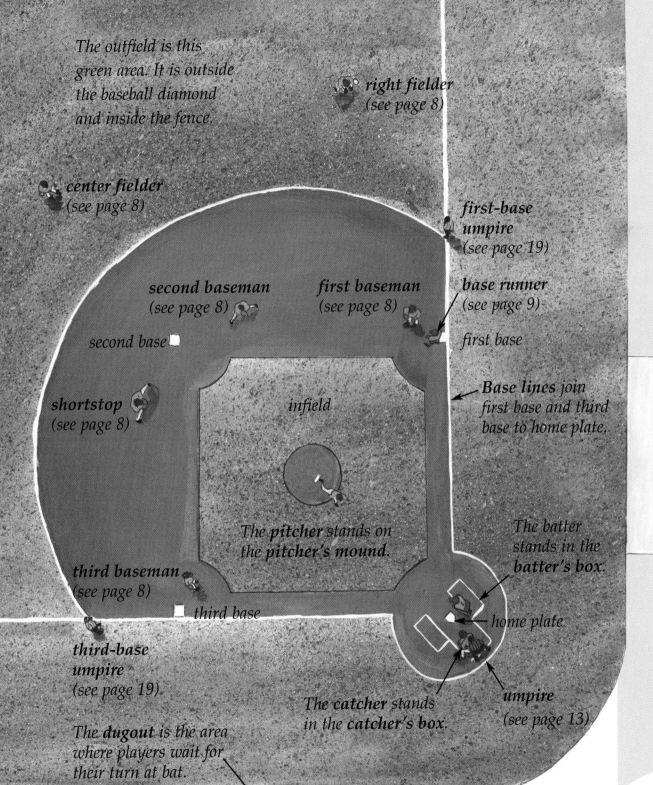

The outfield is this green area. It is outside the baseball diamond and inside the fence.

right fielder
(see page 8)

center fielder
(see page 8)

first-base umpire
(see page 19)

second baseman
(see page 8)

first baseman
(see page 8)

base runner
(see page 9)

second base

first base

shortstop
(see page 8)

infield

Base lines join first base and third base to home plate.

The **pitcher** stands on the **pitcher's mound**.

The **batter** stands in the **batter's box**.

third baseman
(see page 8)

third base

home plate

third-base umpire
(see page 19)

The **catcher** stands in the **catcher's box**.

umpire
(see page 13)

The **dugout** is the area where players wait for their turn at bat.

The players

When a team is fielding, seven players **cover** different areas of the field. To cover means to catch balls that are hit or thrown into that area of the field. The fielding players are either **outfielders** or **infielders**. Outfielders cover the outfield. Infielders cover the infield. The pitcher and the catcher are the two other fielding players (see pages 10-11).

Ins and outs

Three outfielders cover the outfield. They are the left fielder, the center fielder, and the right fielder. Four infielders cover the infield. They are the first baseman, the second baseman, the third baseman, and the shortstop.

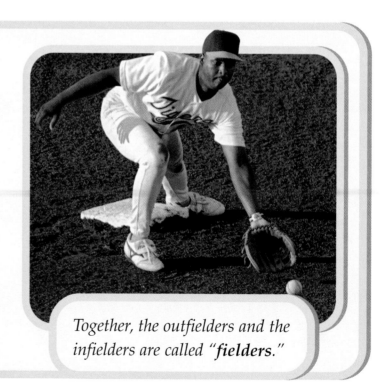

Together, the outfielders and the infielders are called "fielders."

Batting players

When a team is batting, players take turns at bat. The player who is trying to hit the ball is called the batter. The batting team may also have base runners on the field. A base runner is a player who has hit the ball and has made it to a base without getting out.

This player has made it safely to first base. She is now a base runner.

Pitching the ball

The pitcher's job is to **pitch**, or throw, the ball. He throws the ball over home plate toward the catcher. He tries to pitch the ball through the **strike zone**. The strike zone is the area over home plate that is between the batter's chest and his knees (see page 12).

Greg Maddux is a pitcher. He is about to pitch the ball.

Behind home plate

The catcher crouches behind the batter. She uses hand signals to tell the pitcher which pitches to throw. If the batter does not hit the ball, the catcher catches it. After catching the ball, the catcher throws it back to the pitcher.

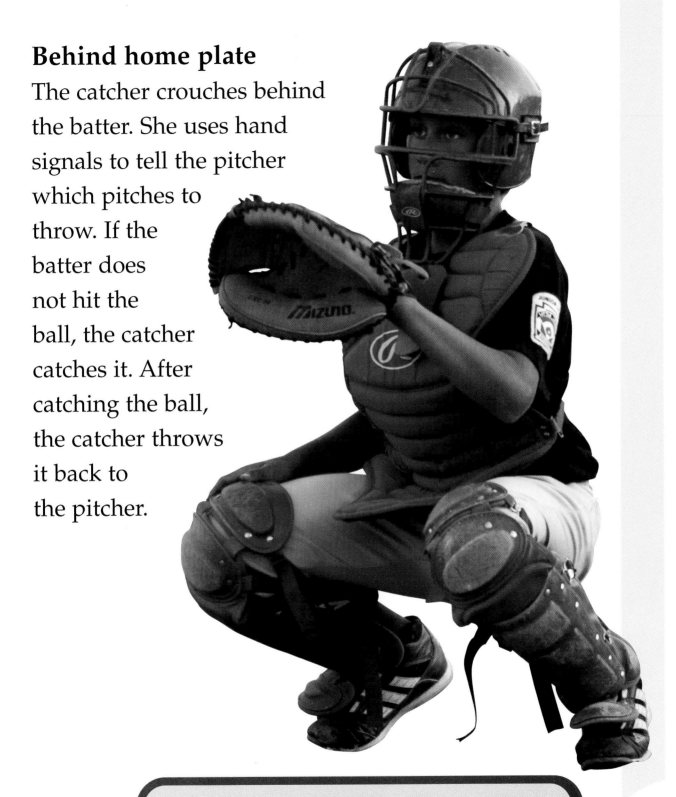

*Together, the pitcher and the catcher are called the **battery**.*

At bat

strike zone

The players on the batting team take turns batting. A batter tries to swing only at pitches that are in the strike zone.

You're out!

If a batter does not swing at a pitch that is in the strike zone, the pitch is called a **strike**. If the batter swings and misses the ball, the pitch is also called a strike. When the batter gets three strikes, he has a **strikeout**. When a batter gets a strikeout, his turn at bat is over.

Ball one, ball two

If a pitcher throws a pitch outside the strike zone, the batter shouldn't swing at it. If the batter doesn't swing, the pitch is called a **ball**. If a pitcher throws four balls, the batter can go to first base without hitting the ball. Going to first base without hitting is called a **walk**.

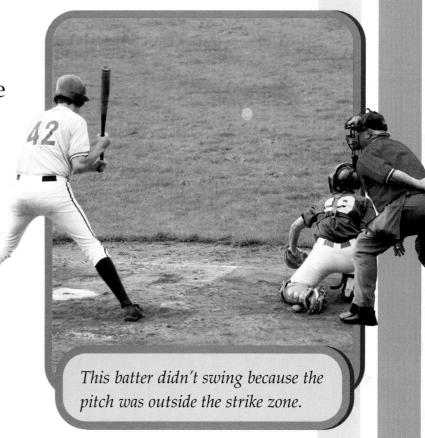

This batter didn't swing because the pitch was outside the strike zone.

Hey, ump!

The umpire is the person who makes sure all the players follow the rules of the game. He stands behind the catcher. There, he can see if a pitch is a ball or a strike. He **calls** "ball" or "strike."

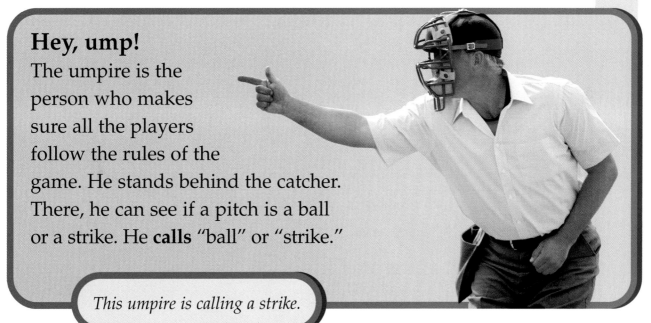

This umpire is calling a strike.

It's a hit!

When a batter hits the ball, he drops the bat and runs toward first base. If the batter makes it safely to first base, he becomes a base runner. A base runner is also called a **runner**.

Types of hits

If the batter makes it to first base, the hit is called a **single**. If the batter hits the ball far enough, he may make it to second base. A second-base hit is called a **double**. A player who hits the ball far into the outfield and makes it to third base has hit a **triple**. A player who touches all the bases and gets back to home plate has hit a **home run**.

This base runner (in white) is running from third base to home plate.

Nice catch!

When a batter hits a ball, the fielders run and try to catch it. If a fielder catches the ball before it hits the ground, the batter is out. This out is called a **fly out**. If the ball hits the ground, the fielder picks it up and throws it to another fielder. A ball that hits the ground before a fielder catches it is called a **ground ball**.

*This outfielder caught a **fly ball**. The batter who hit the ball is now out.*

The ground out

A fielder who picks up a ground ball throws the ball to a baseman. The fielder throws the ball to the baseman who is closest to the runner. If the runner is heading toward first base, the fielder throws the ball to the first baseman. The first baseman catches the ball and touches the base. If she touches the base before the runner gets there, the runner is out. This out is called a **ground out**.

This first baseman is touching first base as she catches the ball. The runner is out because she hasn't yet reached first base.

On the run

A runner who makes it to a base waits for a chance to run to the next base. If a batter hits the ball, the runner can run or stay on the base. The runner must decide if she can get to the next base before the fielders get the ball.

Moving on

Two runners can't stay on one base. For example, a runner may be on second base with a teammate on first base. If a batter hits the ball, both the first-base and second-base runners must move to the next bases, so the batter can run to first base. This runner must head toward the next base. Her teammate has hit the ball.

Tag out

If a runner is not on a base and a fielder touches him with the ball, he is out. This out is called a **tag out**. There is a **base umpire** at each base. Base umpires decide whether a runner is out or **safe**. A player is safe if he has made it to a base without being tagged out.

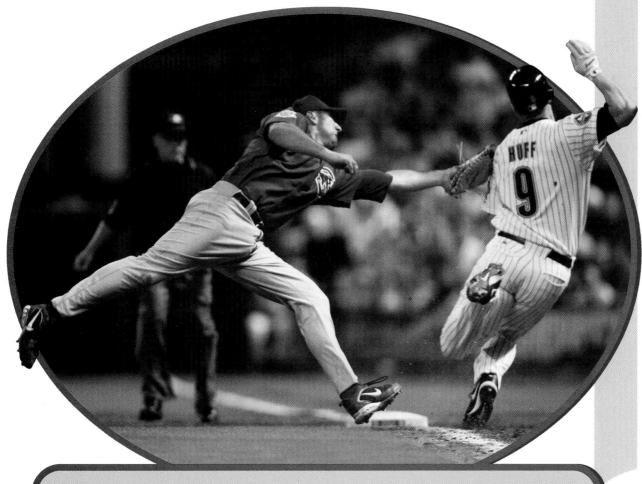

The baseman has touched this runner with the ball. The runner is tagged out!

Stealing bases

A runner may try to run to the next base before a batter hits the ball. This move is called **stealing a base**. To steal a base, the runner waits until the pitcher starts to pitch. The runner then runs as fast as possible toward the next base.

While stealing a base, a runner often slides feet first into the next base.

A head start

Sometimes a base runner takes a **lead off**. A runner takes a lead off by moving a few steps toward the next base before a pitch is thrown. When a runner takes a lead off, he has a head start on reaching the next base. A runner must be careful not to move too far away from the base, however. He could be tagged out if the pitcher suddenly throws the ball to a nearby baseman!

This base runner (on the right) has taken a lead off from first base.

Getting home

Each runner who makes it safely to home plate scores a run. A runner can be tagged out before making it safely to home plate, however. If a runner is tagged out at home plate, he or she is usually tagged out by the catcher.

This runner has been tagged out by the catcher.

Grand slam!

A **grand slam** happens when a team scores four runs at once. A grand slam is a home run that is hit when the bases are **loaded**. The bases are loaded when there is a runner on every base. When a batter hits a grand slam, the batter and the runners on first base, second base, and third base all score runs.

23

Baseball leagues

Most baseball teams are part of a **league**. A league is a group of teams. The teams play games mainly against one another.

The top level

Major League Baseball is the top level of baseball. It is made up of two leagues. The two leagues are the **National League** and the **American League**. There are sixteen teams in the National League and fourteen teams in the American League. Only male baseball players play for Major League Baseball teams. There are no **professional** leagues for women.

Ryan Howard plays for a National League team called the Philadelphia Phillies.

The Minors

Minor League Baseball is made up of twenty leagues. A total of 246 teams belong to these leagues. Players on Minor League teams are training to join Major League teams. Not all Minor League players end up on Major League teams, however. Only the very best players from Minor League teams are asked to join Major League teams.

Justin Leone is a Minor League Baseball player.

The World Series

The **World Series** is the final **championship** of Major League Baseball. At the end of the **season**, the four best teams from both the American League and the National League play in the **playoffs**.

The playoffs

In the playoffs, the American League teams play against one another, and the National League teams play against one another. The American League team that wins the most games becomes the **American League Champion**. The National League team that wins the most games becomes the **National League Champion**.

Justin Morneau plays for the Minnesota Twins. This team played against the Oakland Athletics in the 2006 playoffs.

Best of the best

The World Series takes place each year in October. In the World Series, the American League Champion and the National League Champion play against each other. The team that wins four games out of seven in the World Series becomes the World Series Champion.

Albert Pujols is the first baseman for the St. Louis Cardinals. He helped his team win the World Series in 2006.

Baseball stars

The names of baseball legends are known around the world. They include Joe DiMaggio, Babe Ruth, Mickey Mantle, Cy Young, Reggie Jackson, and many others. Some of today's greatest baseball stars are shown on these pages.

Greg Maddux

Greg Maddux is one of the greatest pitchers of all time. He plays for the Los Angeles Dodgers. Maddux has helped win more than 300 games. He has also made more than 3,000 players strike out!

Derek Jeter

Derek Jeter, shown right, is the shortstop for the New York Yankees. Jeter has helped the Yankees win four World Series Championships.

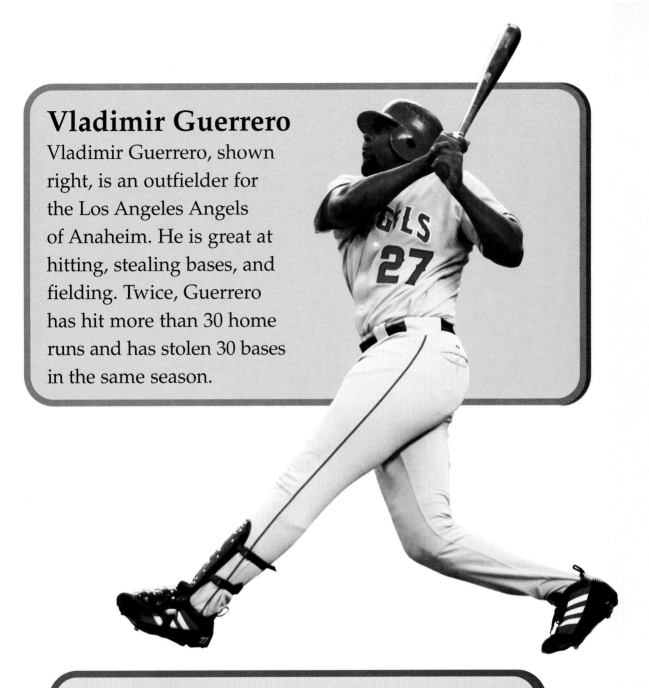

Vladimir Guerrero

Vladimir Guerrero, shown right, is an outfielder for the Los Angeles Angels of Anaheim. He is great at hitting, stealing bases, and fielding. Twice, Guerrero has hit more than 30 home runs and has stolen 30 bases in the same season.

Albert Pujols

Albert Pujols is a strong hitter and first baseman for the St. Louis Cardinals. He hit at least 30 home runs every year for the first six years he played in the Major Leagues. He was the first player ever to do so.

Join a team

If you would like to play baseball, you can join a team at your school or community center. Your hometown likely has a **Little League** team. Little League is a league for young players. More than three million players in over 100 countries play on Little League teams.

These players play on Little League teams.

Other ball games

Softball and **teeball** are games that are similar to baseball. Softballs are larger than baseballs are. Also, a softball diamond is smaller than a baseball diamond is. In teeball, the batter swings at a ball resting on a **tee**, or a post. Playing teeball is a great way to learn how to bat before playing softball or baseball.

This boy is playing teeball.

Glossary

Note: Boldfaced words that are defined in the text may not appear in the glossary.

base A bag at one of three corners of a baseball diamond

batter A player who is trying to hit a ball

call A decision made by an umpire

catcher The player who catches pitches thrown by the pitcher

championship A contest held to decide which team is best in a sport

fly ball A ball that is hit high into the air

home plate The base that a player must reach to score a run

making outs The act of ending a batter's turn

pitcher The player who throws the ball toward the batter

professional A player who is paid to play a sport

season A period of time during which a sport is played

Index

Printed in the U.S.A.